From the Hand of the Penman

Nicholas Dewayne Gillespie

North Mississippi Baptist Bible Institute

Five Pillar Publishing

The Penman Preacher

Copyright Page:

From the Hand of the Penman

Published by
Five Pillar Publishing
Established 2026
503 Woodward Street
Amory, Mississippi 38821
Bulk Orders & Ministry Needs
Five Pillar Publishing titles are available at special quantity discounts for churches, ministries, educational institutions, and conferences. For information, contact the publisher at the address above.
Scripture quotations are taken from the Holy Bible, King James Version (KJV).
Additional study references from The Rock of Ages Study Bible, Second Edition.

ISBN: 979-8-218-93762-1
Library of Congress Control Number: 2026903704
Printed in the United States of America
First Edition: February 2026

Dedication:

This book is dedicated to the faithful men and women who believed the Word of God was worth teaching carefully and preaching boldly.

To my parents, whose patience and instruction shaped my earliest understanding of truth.

To my pastor, who opened a door for a young preacher and trusted him to stand behind a sacred desk.

And to every man called to handle the Word — may you never forget the weight of what rests in your hands.

Acknowledgments:

No minister stands alone. Whatever faithfulness may be found in these pages has been strengthened by the influence of many others.

To my instructors at North Mississippi Baptist Bible Institute — Brothers Don Smith, Kevin Merritt, and Ronnie Barefield — thank you for grounding me in the Scriptures and reminding me that sound doctrine is not optional.

To my parents, Debbie and Paul Gillespie — your guidance, correction, and encouragement laid a foundation long before I ever stepped into a pulpit.

To my pastor and his wife, Brother Joey and Mrs. Dianne Goodwin — thank you for giving me opportunity when I needed experience, and confidence when I needed courage.

To my instructor and dear friend, Brother Bryan Richardson — thank you for sharpening my understanding and challenging me to handle truth precisely.

To Brother Dean Allen and Brother Thomas Stacey — thank you for ministering to me through the Spirit and encouraging steadfastness.

To Mrs. Sherry Prestage — your words of encouragement carried more weight than you know.

To my church family and the many friends who have walked beside me in ordinary moments and long conversations — your fellowship has strengthened this journey.

If there is any clarity here, it is because many hands helped steady the pen.

Author's Note:

At the beginning of each chapter, you will find a personal letter written directly from my heart to yours. These letters are not written from a pedestal, but from the study desk and the prayer closet. They are not criticisms, but exhortations. They are not rebukes, but reminders.

If the tone at times feels searching, remember that it is written with the tenderness of a shepherd and the urgency of a watchman.

May you receive them in that spirit.

Table of Contents:

Foreword:

Hi, my name is Bro. Bryan Richardson. I first met Nick Gillespie almost 14 years ago when he surrendered to preach the gospel during a revival meeting at Gattman First Baptist Church. From there, the Lord would birth a friendship that would lead to us being classmates at NMBBI (North Mississippi Baptist Bible Institute), me becoming his pastor, and eventually him becoming my assistant.

It is during these 14 years that I have been blessed to learn the heart of Bro. Nick Gillespie. Many times during the last 14 years I have heard him speak out of the abundance of his heart, as spoken of in Luke 6:45 and Matthew 12:34. However, as he spoke, his heart was inditing a good matter, and his tongue became the pen of a ready writer, as spoken of in Psalm 45:1.

From there, From the Hand of the Penman was birthed. And it is now my honor, as his friend, pastor, and mentor, to highly recommend this book, From the Hand of the Penman, to you. I pray the words of the penman bless you as they have me.

Friend, Pastor, and Mentor,
Bro. Bryan Richardson

Introduction:

There are seasons in ministry when a man believes he understands more than he truly does. Zeal often arrives before depth. Confidence sometimes precedes formation. And while God is merciful in those early days, time has a way of refining both motives and methods.

This work was not written from a place of arrival, but from reflection. The longer I have served in ministry, the more I have recognized that preaching is not sustained by talent, nor strengthened by personality. It is formed in surrender, shaped in private obedience, and supported by truths that are far older than the preacher who proclaims them.

Each chapter that follows grew out of lessons learned slowly. Some were learned through study. Others through correction. Still others through the quiet realization that effort alone cannot produce spiritual substance. The metaphors used throughout this book—mining for gold, lining up crosshairs, incense on the altar, travail before birth—are not creative devices for their own sake. They are illustrations that helped me understand what God was teaching me about the sacred task of preaching.

This book is written as one continuous exhortation. It is not merely about sermon preparation, but about spiritual posture. It is not simply about delivering messages, but about being formed by the Message before attempting to speak it. The preacher must be supported by something stronger than enthusiasm and anchored in something deeper than preference, or he will not endure.

Ultimately, this work rests under a banner that has upheld the Church for centuries: Scripture as our authority, faith as our means of reception, grace as our provision, Christ as our center, and the glory of God as our end. These truths are not innovations. They are foundations.

What follows, then, is not instruction from above, but encouragement from alongside. It is written as a reminder that the man who stands behind the sacred desk must first kneel before the Lord who called him there.

CHAPTER 1: PREACHING IN PERSPECTIVE

Are You Panning For Gold Or Are You Tapping The Vein?

Dear Man (or Woman) of God,

I write this not to dictate how you or your pastor should preach, but to remind you that every faithful style of preaching has its place within the sovereign design of God. The Lord has always used different voices, different temperaments, and different structures to accomplish His purpose. There comes a defining moment in every preacher's life when he must decide whether he will allow God to shape him according to divine intention, or whether he will attempt to shape himself after other men he admires. It is often in that quiet internal struggle that discouragement presses in the hardest. In that moment, encouragement is not a luxury — it is a necessity.

The Lord told Jeremiah, "Before I formed thee in the belly I knew thee." That truth anchors every called servant. You are not an accident. You are not a copy. You are not a substitute standing in for someone more

gifted. You are a called identity, formed intentionally by God for a specific people and a specific season. Do not cheat yourself — or your church — by trying to become the next "Joe Somebody." God did not call you to replicate another man's cadence, outline structure, or delivery style. He called you to be you, refined by His Word and governed by His Spirit.

With love from above,
The Penman Preacher

Finding the Nugget:

It may sound like an unusual analogy, but preaching is much like mining for gold. When a preacher opens the Word of God, he is not merely scanning literature or assembling religious thoughts; he is prospecting for eternal treasure. Many sermons remain shallow because the preacher never truly digs beneath the surface. He reads, he gathers a thought, he forms a quick outline, and he moves on. But gold is rarely found by those unwilling to labor.

Consider John 3:16: "For God so loved the world, that he gave his only begotten Son..." A preacher might discover a simple nugget in two words: "He gave." Yet those two words carry immeasurable weight. Everything we possess in Christ rests upon that divine act of giving. Because He gave, I have a Savior. Because He gave, I am forgiven. Because He gave, I have a home in Heaven. That small phrase contains a universe of grace. The nugget is not merely information for the mind; it is transformation for the soul.

Yet nuggets found in riverbeds are fragments broken from something larger. They are evidence of a deeper deposit upstream. If the preacher stops with the nugget alone, he may preach something true, stirring, and even helpful — but he will not mine the depth of the passage. The faithful preacher must learn to ask a second question beyond "What shines?" He must ask, "Where is the vein from which this truth flows?"

Tapping the Vein:

Surface reading may provide inspiration. Careful study will reveal literary structure. But disciplined meditation — the slow turning of the text in the heart — uncovers the vein. The vein is the sustained doctrinal current running beneath the text. It is the unifying theology that supports and explains the passage. It connects the immediate words to the larger revelation of Scripture.

When a preacher taps the vein, he begins to see context within the chapter, continuity within the book, and coherence within the whole canon. He sees how the passage connects to Christ and how application must be grounded in doctrine rather than preference. The sermon becomes anchored rather than improvised. It becomes weighty rather than merely energetic.

Anyone can find a nugget with minimal effort. Faithful preachers, however, discipline themselves to mine until they discover the vein. Depth is rarely accidental. It is cultivated through prayerful persistence.

Four Styles of Faithful Preaching

Throughout church history, God has used various faithful approaches to proclaim His truth. Terminology may vary, but four broad categories commonly appear. Expository preaching explains the meaning of a text in its immediate context and follows the structure of the passage itself. Doctrinal preaching systematically presents biblical truth around a particular theological theme. Textual preaching develops key truths directly from a specific portion of Scripture, often organizing points drawn explicitly from the text. Topical preaching gathers and organizes multiple passages around a central subject in order to present a comprehensive biblical perspective.

Each approach has value when handled responsibly. The danger is not found in the style itself, but in imbalance or misuse. Style must always serve substance. Structure must always serve Scripture. When form begins to dominate faithfulness, authority weakens. The goal is not to defend a method, but to faithfully deliver the Word of God.

The Hermeneutical Framework:

Faithful preaching does not begin with creativity; it begins with submission. Before outlining a sermon, the preacher must wrestle honestly with the text. What does the passage actually say? What did it mean to its original audience? How does it fit within the unfolding story of redemption? In what way does it point to Christ, reflect Christ, or depend upon Christ? What timeless truth does it declare? What response does it demand from believers and unbelievers alike?

An outline must rise naturally from the text rather than being imposed upon it. When a preacher forces personal ideas into a passage, he may still sound compelling, but he undermines spiritual authority. True authority does not come from volume, personality, or clever phrasing. Authority flows from rightly handled Scripture.

The Preacher of Preachers:

Every faithful preacher ultimately follows the pattern of Christ Himself. He opened the Scriptures and explained them plainly. He fulfilled them in His own person and applied them directly to the hearts of His hearers. He never manipulated emotion to compensate for weak truth. He spoke with authority because He was truth incarnate.

We do not possess inherent authority as He did. Yet we may faithfully echo His authority when we submit ourselves to His Word. The more clearly we proclaim what God has said, the more confidently we may speak.

Pastoral Charge:

Brother and sister in Christ, your voice matters — not because it is yours, but because God entrusted it to you. Do not despise structure, for clarity honors your hearers. Do not idolize style, for personality fades but truth endures. Do not imitate other preachers at the expense of authenticity. Study deeply until conviction settles in your own heart. Pray earnestly until pride is pressed out. Preach faithfully whether applause follows or not.

Gold is not found by accident. Neither is spiritual power. Ask yourself regularly: Am I content with surface nuggets, or am I pressing toward the vein that sustains lasting truth?

Expanded Study Guide:

Set aside intentional time for self-examination. Write your answers thoughtfully rather than responding mentally.

Consider which preaching style most naturally describes your current approach and why. Evaluate whether you tend to default to inspirational thoughts instead of careful interpretation. Reflect on whether prayer or outline construction receives priority in your preparation process. Ask yourself honestly if you have ever shaped a passage to fit a preferred idea rather than allowing it to speak for itself.

Estimate how much of your preparation time is spent observing the text compared to developing application. Remember the last time a passage corrected, rebuked, or humbled you personally before you preached it to others. Examine whether you feel subtle pressure to imitate another preacher's tone, pace, or expressions. Finally, assess whether you are mining consistently each week or only when circumstances are convenient. In at least two hundred words, write where you are faithfully mining and where you may be settling for surface-level nuggets. This written reflection will reveal patterns that casual thinking may conceal.

Text Work Drill:

Choose a passage of five to ten verses and move deliberately through four stages. Begin with observation by listing repeated words, identifying the main verb that drives the passage, and noting transitions, contrasts, or connecting phrases. Do not rush this stage. Careful observation prevents careless interpretation.

Proceed to interpretation by summarizing the central idea of the text in one clear past-tense sentence. Then identify the doctrinal truth that undergirds the passage — the theological vein that supports the visible nugget. After interpretation, establish the Christ connection. Ask whether the text anticipates Christ prophetically, reflects His character, flows from His finished work, or depends upon His ongoing ministry.

Only after these steps should you move to application. Determine what believers must believe, confess, repent of, or obey in light of this truth. Clarify what the lost must understand about God, sin, righteousness, or grace. Do not move to illustration until interpretation is settled. Illustration without interpretation produces excitement without foundation.

Group Discussion (For Bible Institute or Preacher Fellowship):

Discuss the practical dangers of nugget-only preaching and how it may unintentionally weaken doctrinal stability within a congregation. Explore how structure, rather than restricting the Spirit, can provide clarity that strengthens Spirit-led preaching. Reflect on why security in one's calling is essential for authenticity in the pulpit. Consider practical safeguards against stylistic imitation and identify habits that cultivate deeper mining of Scripture. Finally, discuss how to balance doctrinal depth with congregational clarity so that truth remains both weighty and understandable.

Sermon Development Workshop:

For vein identification, select a short passage and write the full text before you. Craft an ETS (Essence of the Text) in one past-tense sentence summarizing what the passage meant. Then write an ESS (Essence of the Sermon) in one present-tense sentence stating what the truth means now. Develop a clear OSS (Objective of the Sermon Statement) that defines the intended response. Identify one doctrinal vein beneath the text and one clear Christ-centered fulfillment. Ensure that every movement of your outline grows naturally from the passage itself.

Conduct a surface versus depth audit on a recent sermon. Ask whether you defined key terms, explained historical and literary context, connected doctrinal implications, and demonstrated how the passage fits into the larger biblical narrative. Consider whether the sermon could have been transferred to another text with minimal revision. If so, you may have handled a nugget rather than the sustaining vein.

Finally, complete an identity check. Write privately whose preaching style most influences you, what specific qualities you admire, and what elements you feel tempted to imitate. Then identify the distinct strengths, burdens, and gifts God has entrusted to you. Pray specifically for contentment in your calling and courage to develop your own faithful voice.

Prayer Focus:

Father, guard me from shallow study and hurried preparation. Lord Jesus, let every text I handle lead me clearly to You. Holy Spirit, teach me to labor in the Word until I find treasure beneath the surface. Protect me from imitation that dishonors my calling and from pride that distorts Your truth. Help me tap the vein, not merely gather scattered nuggets. Amen.

CHAPTER 2: CRUCIFIXION

THE SCARLET THREAD OF THE BIBLE

Dear Man (or Woman) of God,

I write to encourage you in a season that demands clarity and courage. As we draw closer to the return of our Lord and Savior Jesus Christ, we must continue standing boldly for the cross of Christ without hesitation or apology. In many churches across our nation, the cross is no longer central. It has been minimized, softened, reframed, or in some cases quietly removed from emphasis altogether. Much like the days of Elijah when he confronted the prophets of Baal at Mount Carmel, we are witnessing a time when the altar of the Lord lies in disrepair. The structure may remain, the language may remain, the programs may remain, but the fire has diminished because the altar has not been carefully maintained. It is time to rebuild the altar. Place the cross of Jesus Christ back where it belongs — at the center of proclamation and theology. Set the sacrifice in order. Apply the washing of the water of the Word. Pray for divine intervention. And I believe with all my heart that we will see the fire fall again.

With Love From Above,
The Penman Preacher

The Scarlet Thread Begins:

The cross did not begin in Bethlehem, nor did it originate at Golgotha. It began in the heart of God before the foundation of the world. From Genesis to Revelation, a scarlet thread runs through Scripture — a line of blood, promise, sacrifice, and substitution — all converging at Calvary. The Bible is not a collection of disconnected moral lessons; it is a unified revelation of redemption. If you remove the cross, the Bible begins to unravel. If you silence the blood, redemption collapses under the weight of human effort. If you soften Calvary, Christianity is reduced to morality without power. The scarlet thread is not an embellishment of Scripture; it is its structural integrity.

The First Shadow — Genesis 3

After Adam and Eve sinned, shame entered their experience. Fear followed swiftly behind. Fellowship with God fractured under the weight of rebellion. When confronted with guilt, they attempted to cover themselves with fig leaves — a human solution to a spiritual problem. Yet God did not respond with self-help instruction or therapeutic reassurance. He responded with sacrifice. Scripture records, "Unto Adam also and to his wife did the LORD God make coats of skins, and clothed them." Something died so they could be covered. Innocent blood was shed to cover guilty shame. In that moment, the first shadow of substitution appeared. The scarlet thread had begun to weave its way through history.

The Pattern of Substitution:

As the Old Testament unfolds, the pattern becomes unmistakable. Abel's offering was accepted because it involved blood, acknowledging both guilt and need for atonement. Abraham's ram was provided "in the stead of his son," demonstrating substitution in vivid clarity. The Passover lamb in Egypt shielded households from judgment when its blood was applied according to divine instruction. The Day of Atonement required blood upon the mercy seat, emphasizing that access to God demanded sacrificial provision. Every altar, every lamb, every priestly act whispered the same unchanging truth: without shedding of blood is no remission. The cross is not a New Testament innovation. It is the fulfillment of a long-established Old Testament pattern ordained by God.

The Prophetic Anticipation:

The prophets did not merely predict national restoration; they foresaw suffering. Isaiah declared, "He was wounded for our transgressions, he was bruised for our iniquities." This was not poetic exaggeration; it was prophetic precision. The coming Messiah would not only reign — He would bleed. He would bear grief, carry sorrow, and be stricken for sins not His own. The cross was not an interruption of God's plan, nor was it a tragic accident in history. It was the centerpiece of divine redemption, foreknown and foretold long before Roman nails pierced sacred flesh.

The Historical Reality:

When Christ came, He did not come merely to teach ethical principles or model compassion. He came to die. John the Baptist announced His arrival with unmistakable clarity: "Behold the Lamb of God, which taketh away the sin of the world." Lamb language is sacrificial language. At Calvary, the scarlet thread reached its crimson climax. The innocent died for the guilty. The Just suffered for the unjust. Wrath fell — not upon sinners directly — but upon the willing Substitute who stood in their place. This is not sentimental theology designed to stir emotion; it is substitutionary atonement grounded in divine justice and mercy.

The Doctrine of the Cross:

To preach the cross faithfully, we must explain it clearly and thoroughly. The cross reveals the holiness of God, because sin required judgment and could not be dismissed casually. It reveals the seriousness of sin, because if sin could have been overlooked cheaply, Calvary would have been unnecessary. It reveals the justice of God, because He did not ignore sin but judged it fully. It reveals the love of God, because He bore that judgment Himself in the person of His Son. It reveals the sufficiency of Christ, because "It is finished" was not a sigh of defeat but a declaration of completion. The cross is where justice and mercy meet without contradiction. Remove one, and the gospel becomes distorted.

Why the Cross Offends:

The cross confronts human pride at its deepest level. It declares that you cannot save yourself. It insists that you are not mostly good with minor flaws. It exposes that effort is insufficient and religion is inadequate. Modern culture prefers affirmation over atonement and encouragement over conviction. Yet without atonement, there is no reconciliation. Without conviction, there is no repentance. The offense of the cross is not a flaw in the gospel; it is the doorway through which grace enters a humbled heart.

Preaching from the Cross:

There is a vital difference between preaching about the cross and preaching from it. Preaching about the cross mentions it occasionally as a historical event. Preaching from the cross allows every doctrine, every exhortation, and every application to flow from redemptive truth. Not every sermon must carry an overtly evangelistic tone, but every sermon must rest upon the foundation of Christ's finished work. Whether addressing marriage, suffering, holiness, prayer, stewardship, or doctrine, the cross anchors the message in grace and truth. The cross is not a seasonal emphasis reserved for holidays; it is the spine of Scripture and the heartbeat of faithful preaching.

Rebuilding the Altar:

Elijah repaired the altar before he called for fire from heaven. If fire has diminished in our pulpits, we must examine the altar carefully. Have we softened sin to avoid discomfort? Have we minimized wrath to appear culturally sensitive? Have we avoided blood language because it seems offensive? Have we replaced substitution with vague inspiration, or repentance with mere self-improvement? The solution is not louder preaching but restored foundations. Rebuild the altar. Lay the sacrifice in order. Drench it thoroughly with the Word of God. Then pray with expectation. Fire still falls on repaired altars.

Pastoral Charge:

Brother and sister, the cross is not a sermon series to be scheduled; it is the spine of Scripture itself. If the cross is removed, preaching becomes advice. If the blood is silenced, church becomes performance. If Calvary is softened, salvation becomes sentiment without substance. Do not apologize for the cross. Do not dilute the blood. Do not move the altar. Preach Christ crucified — not as an accessory to ministry, but as its center. The scarlet thread is not decorative. It is redemptive, and it must remain visible in every generation.

Expanded Study & Reflection:

Set aside unhurried time for personal examination. Ask yourself whether the cross is central in your preaching calendar or merely occasional. Consider whether you clearly define substitution when you preach it or assume your congregation already understands atonement. Reflect on whether you explain both wrath and mercy with equal clarity. Examine whether you hesitate to use biblical language concerning blood and sacrifice. Determine whether repentance is presented as necessary or optional. Evaluate whether you have ever reduced the cross to emotional appeal rather than doctrinal explanation. Finally, consider whether the cross corrects your own pride regularly before you proclaim it to others. In at least two hundred words, write honestly: if someone listened to your last five sermons, would they hear the cross clearly proclaimed or merely hear it referenced in passing?

Biblical Thread Mapping Exercise:

Trace the scarlet thread through at least five key passages, including Genesis 3, Genesis 22, Exodus 12, Leviticus 16, Isaiah 53, the crucifixion narratives, and Hebrews 9–10. In each passage, identify the sacrificial element and the substitutionary element. Explain how the passage anticipates Christ or clarifies His finished work. Then write one concise sentence directly connecting the passage to Calvary. As you complete this exercise, notice the continuity of divine design and the consistency of redemptive purpose across centuries of revelation.

Group Discussion (For Bible Institute or Preacher Fellowship):

Discuss why modern culture resists the doctrine of blood atonement and how discomfort with wrath influences preaching trends. Examine how emotional manipulation can counterfeit genuine conviction and why doctrinal clarity protects against such distortion. Consider what happens theologically when wrath is ignored or minimized. Reflect on how tracing the scarlet thread strengthens confidence in the unity and authority of Scripture. Finally, explore the difference between inspiration and substitution, and discuss how to preach repentance faithfully without unnecessary harshness or pride.

Sermon Development Workshop:

For the exercise of tracing the thread, select one Old Testament passage that foreshadows Christ and identify the type or shadow within it. Then locate its fulfillment in the New Testament and state clearly the doctrinal truth revealed. Write an ETS (Essence of the Text) in fifteen words or fewer, craft a present-tense ESS (Essence of the Sermon), and develop a clear OSS defining what the hearer must believe or do. Ensure that the cross is not merely implied but openly declared.

From Galatians 3:13, define the curse, explain substitution in plain language, and demonstrate the reversal accomplished in Christ. Provide one application for believers and one invitation for the lost. Ask yourself honestly whether you explained redemption carefully or merely celebrated it emotionally.

Finally, take a recent sermon you preached and identify where the cross appeared within it. Determine whether it functioned as foundational truth or supplemental reference.

Ask whether the sermon could stand without Calvary. If it could stand without the cross, rebuild it until redemption is unmistakable.

Prayer Focus:

Father, keep the altar repaired in my heart before I step into any pulpit. Lord Jesus, never let me grow cold toward Your sacrifice or casual about Your suffering. Holy Spirit, grant me courage to preach the blood without apology and clarity to explain it without confusion. Guard me from softening truth for approval and from preaching sentiment instead of substance. Let the fire fall again — beginning with me. Amen.

CHAPTER 3: TYPES & ANTITYPES

FROM THE TABERNACLE TO THE TEMPLE

Dear Man (or Woman) of God,

Have you ever paused over certain passages of Scripture and wondered why events unfolded exactly as they did? Have detailed descriptions of measurements, fabrics, metals, and ceremonies ever caused you to ask the Lord quietly, "What does this mean?" Those moments are not accidents. They are invitations to look deeper. In preparation for this chapter, I revisited the writings of Clarence Larkin, a faithful student of dispensational truth and biblical typology whose work has sharpened generations of Bible readers. What you are about to read is not an attempt to copy his labor, but rather a testimony to the influence of a teacher whose insights encouraged me to study more carefully and trace Scripture more faithfully.

In this chapter we will examine how the Old Testament reveals Jesus Christ in shadow, symbol, and structure, and how the New Testament unfolds what was concealed. We will act as wise "householders," bringing forth treasures both new and old, carefully following the Scarlet Thread that runs through Scripture. The New is in the Old contained, and the

Old is by the New explained. When teaching remains ordered and disciplined, we discover that through Scripture alone we see Christ alone. Salvation is by grace alone, through faith alone, and to God alone be the glory.

With Love From Above,
The Penman Preacher

The Householder's Treasure: Unfolding the Shadows

As teachers of the Word, we are called to function as wise householders who bring out of their treasure things new and old, as our Lord described in Matthew 13:52. The "old" things are the types and shadows embedded in the Old Testament. The "new" things are their fulfillment in the person and work of Christ. The Old Testament enfolds truth in shadow, often presenting realities in symbolic form. The New Testament unfolds those same truths in substance and clarity. Augustine summarized this relationship well when he wrote, "The New is in the Old contained; the Old is by the New explained." When we follow the Scarlet Thread carefully, we begin to see that every intentional shadow points forward to Christ. The Tabernacle was not merely a portable structure erected in the wilderness. It was a sermon constructed of wood, fabric, metal, oil, and blood — preaching silently of a coming Redeemer.

The Theme of the Coverings: Inward Glory and Outward Humility

Before entering the Tabernacle itself, we must consider its coverings, for they reveal profound truth concerning both the humility and the hidden glory of Christ. The outermost covering of badger skins was weather-resistant and practical, yet visually unimpressive. To the natural eye, it carried little beauty or attraction. This reflects Christ's outward appearance to the world. Isaiah 53:2 reminds us that there was no form or comeliness that would cause men to desire Him. To the unbelieving eye, there was nothing spectacular about the carpenter from Nazareth. The glory was veiled.

Beneath that layer lay the ram skins dyed red. The ram in Scripture is closely associated with substitution, most memorably in Genesis 22. The red-dyed skins speak unmistakably of sacrifice and applied blood. Here we see the obedient Servant who humbled Himself unto death, fulfilling the pattern long established in shadow.

Below that was the covering of goat's hair. The goat was the animal of the sin offering, especially on the Day of Atonement. In this covering we see the shadow of Christ being made sin for us, though He knew no sin. The sinless One assumed the place of the guilty.

Finally, the innermost covering of fine twined linen, embroidered with cherubim in blue, purple, and scarlet, was visible only from within. It represents Christ in His essential purity — divine, royal, and sinless. Only those who entered could behold its beauty. What a portrait is presented: outward humility concealing inward glory.

The Theme of the Branch and the Four Colors

Access to God required passage through the gate of the court, woven with blue, purple, scarlet, and fine white linen. These colors were not decorative accidents. They reveal the fourfold presentation of Christ as seen in the Gospels. Blue speaks of the Divine Branch, "the Branch of the LORD" in Isaiah 4:2, unfolded in John as the Word made flesh. Purple reflects the Kingly Branch described in Zechariah 6:12–13, unfolded in Matthew where Christ is presented as King. Scarlet points to the Servant Branch of Zechariah 3:8, unfolded in Mark as the suffering Servant who gives His life. Fine white linen corresponds to the Human Branch, "Behold the man," also in Zechariah, unfolded in Luke as the perfect Man. Even before sacrifice was offered, the gate itself preached Christ in color and composition.

The Theme of the Sacrifices: The Work of the Savior

At the Brazen Altar, shadow meets substance most vividly. The Levitical offerings were not redundant rituals but carefully designed portraits of Calvary. The sin and trespass offerings addressed both sinful nature and specific sinful acts, and Christ suffered outside the gate as our substitute, fulfilling what those sacrifices anticipated. The burnt offering symbolized total consecration and complete surrender, and Christ offered Himself wholly as a sweet-smelling savor unto God. The grain offering, composed of fine flour mingled with oil and without leaven, portrays Christ's sinless character — holy, harmless, undefiled. The peace offering spoke of reconciliation and restored fellowship, made possible only through the blood of His cross. Each offering reveals a distinct facet of the cross, and together they form a unified testimony to the sufficiency of Christ's work.

The Theme of the Furniture: The Path to the Presence

The arrangement of the Tabernacle furniture outlines the believer's approach to God. The Brazen Altar and the Laver remind us of justification by blood and sanctification through the washing of water by the Word. Beyond them, the Table of Shewbread presents Christ as the Bread of Life who sustains His people. The Golden Lampstand reveals Him as the Light of the World who illumines darkness. The Altar of Incense portrays the intercessory ministry of our Great High Priest, who ever lives to make intercession for us. Finally, the Ark of the Covenant stands as the focal point of divine presence. Within it rested the Law; above it was the Mercy Seat; upon it was sprinkled the blood. Here we see propitiation — mercy triumphing over judgment because blood has been applied. The furniture does not merely decorate sacred space; it preaches the way into God's presence.

The Theme of the Garments: The Office of the Priest

The High Priest's garments reveal Christ's present ministry. The blue robe, adorned with bells and pomegranates, symbolized testimony and fruitfulness — sound accompanied by life. His ministry is not empty proclamation but effective mediation. The breastplate, containing the Urim and Thummim, signified lights and perfections, and it rested upon the priest's heart, reminding us that Christ carries His people continually before the Father. The mitre bore the inscription "HOLINESS TO THE LORD," declaring absolute purity. Our Mediator is not flawed or partial; He is perfectly holy, representing us without corruption before a holy God.

The Theme of the Feasts: The Prophetic Timeline

The seven feasts of Israel outlined in Leviticus 23 form a prophetic calendar of redemption. The spring feasts — Passover, Unleavened Bread, Firstfruits, and Pentecost — correspond to Christ's death, burial, resurrection, and the coming of the Holy Spirit. The fall feasts — Trumpets, Atonement, and Tabernacles — point toward regathering, national repentance, and millennial rest. Israel's calendar tells redemption's story in ordered progression. What was rehearsed annually in shadow has been and will be fulfilled precisely in substance.

Conclusion: The Unfolding of the Treasure

When each theme is handled carefully and kept distinct, the unfolding becomes beautifully clear. The coverings reveal His person. The colors reveal His character. The sacrifices reveal His work. The furniture reveals His way. The garments reveal His office. The feasts reveal His timing. Through Scripture alone we see Christ alone. By grace alone, through faith alone, we are saved, and to God alone be the glory. The Tabernacle was never merely ancient architecture; it was a shadow of the cross, and every shadow ultimately bows to the Substance — Jesus Christ.

Pastoral Charge;

Brother and sister, typology is not spiritual imagination; it is disciplined, text-governed observation. We must never force Christ into a passage where He is not revealed by the whole counsel of God. At the same time, we must not fail to see Him where Scripture clearly testifies. The shadows were given intentionally, and the substance has now been revealed. Teach carefully. Connect faithfully. Exalt Christ consistently. The Old Testament is not obsolete; it is pregnant with glory and rich with anticipation. Handle it reverently. Trace it patiently. Preach it Christ-centered.

Study & Reflection:

Take time for personal examination. Ask yourself whether you approach Old Testament passages expecting to see Christ revealed through redemptive design. Reflect on whether you have ever confused disciplined typology with creative speculation. Consider whether you clearly distinguish between illustration and fulfillment when teaching. Evaluate whether your preaching responsibly connects Old Testament texts to New Testament revelation while allowing Scripture to interpret Scripture. Examine whether you have neglected difficult passages rather than mining their treasure. Write one thoughtful paragraph answering this question: Am I uncovering treasure, or overlooking it?

Group Discussion:

Discuss the difference between a biblical type grounded in textual continuity and a creative allegory driven by imagination. Consider why structure and order are essential when teaching typology. Reflect on how the themes of the Tabernacle protect teachers from doctrinal imbalance by keeping Christ central. Explore how tracing fulfillment strengthens confidence in the unity and inspiration of Scripture. Finally, discuss practical safeguards against overreaching in symbolic interpretation and why Christ must remain the interpretive center of all redemptive teaching.

Sermon Development Workshop:

Select one Old Testament element — whether person, object, event, or institution — and identify its historical setting and original purpose. Then determine its New Testament fulfillment and state the doctrinal connection clearly and concisely. Write an ETS in fifteen words or fewer and craft a present-tense ESS that communicates enduring truth. Ensure the connection is textual rather than imaginative.

Next, choose one theme from this chapter — coverings, colors, sacrifices, furniture, garments, or feasts — and identify one clear Christological connection, one doctrinal implication, and one pastoral application. Write a short introduction that explains the shadow before proclaiming the substance. Ask yourself honestly whether you explained the shadow sufficiently before revealing its fulfillment in Christ.

Prayer Focus:

Father, open my eyes to behold wondrous things out of Thy law. Lord Jesus, let every shadow lead me to Your substance. Holy Spirit, restrain me from speculation and guide me into truth. Make me a faithful householder, bringing forth treasures both new and old. Let Christ be seen clearly in every shadow I teach. Amen.

CHAPTER 4: QUESTIONS TO ASK

Lining Up Your Crosshairs

Dear Man (or Woman) of God,

Have you ever sensed the Lord giving you a work to do, yet you were not quite sure how to accomplish it? Pastors face this more often than we admit. In sermon preparation, we sometimes forget that God is not only the One who calls us to preach—He is also willing to help us prepare.

When uncertainty arises, step back and think clearly. Ask yourself:

What does the Bible say?
Who am I doing this for?
When am I doing it?
Where am I doing it?
Why am I doing it?
How will it be received?

Just because something can be done—or even seems like a good idea—does not mean it is the right thing to do. Let God lead you, and you cannot go wrong.

With Love From Above,
The Penman Preacher

Sermons Out of Focus

Allow me to begin with counsel learned through experience: avoid preaching out of circumstance. When all you are focusing on is what affects you personally, it may be time to step back and reevaluate. Preaching from wounded emotion or personal frustration can make the difference between building up the house of God and swinging through it like a wrecking ball.

A sermon born merely from irritation may carry volume, but it will lack vision. So how do we line up our crosshairs so that our sermons consistently strike the mark for the Lord?

Any marksman will tell you that a scope has two crosshairs, and both must align properly to hit the target. In preaching, one set belongs to us—our intention, preparation, and delivery. The other belongs to the Lord—His will, His Word, and His Spirit. If they are not aligned, we will miss the mark no matter how passionate we may be.

Alignment is not accidental; it is intentional. Ask yourself these six questions consistently, and you will find your aim improving.

Who? — Who Are You Preaching For?

Notice I said for, not to.

If you preach for the congregation, you risk one of two dangers: either trying to play the "Holy Ghost" by manipulating outcomes, or feeding off your flock rather than feeding your flock. If you preach for yourself, pride will eventually undo you. Stand on a pedestal long enough, and the enemy will gladly knock you off.

But when you preach every message for Jesus Christ, your motive is purified. As Scripture declares, "Whether therefore ye eat, or drink, or whatsoever ye do, do all to the glory of God" (1 Corinthians 10:31). Preaching for Christ steadies the heart, clarifies the motive, and protects the soul from both pride and performance.

What? — What Does the Bible Say?

Too often we become consumed with what we want to say and neglect to communicate what God has already said. Faithful preaching begins with faithful study. We must draw truth from the text rather than force the text to support our ideas.

Paul instructed Timothy, "Study to shew thyself approved unto God... rightly dividing the word of truth" (2 Timothy 2:15). Our authority does not come from personality, creativity, charisma, or volume. It comes from Scripture rightly handled and rightly applied. When the Word speaks, we must decrease so that its voice increases.

When? — When Are You Preparing?

One of my own struggles has been procrastination. If you are preaching Sunday night, Saturday evening is not the ideal time to begin. Preparation is not a lack of faith; it is evidence of faithfulness.

Paul exhorted Timothy, "Preach the word; be instant in season, out of season" (2 Timothy 4:2). Readiness requires discipline. The Spirit may ignite the message in the moment, but discipline prepares the wood for the fire.

A prepared preacher is not less spiritual; he is more dependable. Order invites clarity, and clarity strengthens confidence.

Where? — Where Is Your Congregation Spiritually?

A sermon must be true, but it must also be digestible. You cannot feed an infant a T-bone steak, and you cannot expect an adult to grow on milk alone. A wise shepherd discerns the spiritual maturity of his people and adjusts delivery without adjusting doctrine.

Paul acknowledged this in Corinth when he wrote, "I have fed you with milk, and not with meat" (1 Corinthians 3:2). Depth does not require complexity. Some of the deepest truths in Scripture are communicated most powerfully in simple language. Present what God gives you in a way your people can receive and apply.

Why? — Why This Text?

Are you preaching this passage because you like it? Preference alone is not sinful, but if we only preach our favorite texts, we limit the Spirit's work in us.

Are you preaching it because the congregation prefers it? That may lead to ear-tickling rather than truth.

Are you preaching it because of a recent disagreement or a private frustration? That may turn the pulpit into a weapon rather than a shepherd's staff.

The better question is this: Has God led you here?

Every text has divine authority, but not every text is assigned to you for every moment. Seek the Lord concerning what your people need—not what your emotions demand. If the text was chosen prayerfully rather than impulsively, it will carry a different spirit when preached.

How? — How Will This Be Received?

This question is not asked to soften truth but to clarify delivery. Paul wrote that we are to speak the truth in love (Ephesians 4:15). Truth without love can bruise. Love without truth can mislead.

Consider your tone. Consider your posture. Consider your timing. Ask whether your words are shaped by compassion or sharpened by irritation. The same truth can either heal or harm depending on the spirit in which it is delivered.

We cannot control how every message is received, but we are accountable for how it is delivered.

Bringing the Crosshairs Together

When these six questions align—when you are preaching for Christ, from the Word, with prayerful preparation, mindful of your people, led faithfully through your text, and governed by love—the crosshairs settle. They do not settle on preference, personality, or performance. They settle on truth. And when the crosshairs settle on truth, clarity replaces confusion, conviction replaces noise, and Christ is seen plainly before His people.

The message becomes less about proving a point and more about proclaiming a Person. The pulpit ceases to be a platform for reaction and becomes a place of revelation.

Marksmen adjust their scope carefully because they know the cost of missing the mark. Preachers must adjust their hearts with equal seriousness. The stakes are eternal.

Pastoral Charge

Brother and sister, do not preach in haste. Do not preach in anger. Do not preach in pride.

Ask the questions.
Align the crosshairs.
Submit your intention to the Spirit of God.

Then step into the pulpit with confidence—not because you are certain of yourself, but because you are surrendered to Him.

When your will aligns with His Word, you will not miss the mark.

Study & Reflection

Consider the last three sermons you preached. Which of the six questions received the most attention? Which received the least?

Have you ever chosen a text primarily because of personal frustration? Have you ever avoided a text because of fear of reaction?

Write a paragraph describing a time when your "crosshairs" were misaligned and what you learned from it. Then write another paragraph describing a time when you sensed clear alignment between your preparation and the Spirit's leading. What was different?

Prayer Focus

Father, align my heart with Your will.
Lord Jesus, keep my motive pure and my message clear.
Holy Spirit, correct my aim before I step into the pulpit.
Let me preach for Christ, from Scripture, in love, and for Your glory.
Amen.

CHAPTER 5

INCENSE ON THE ALTAR

Prayer Before You Preach

Dear Man (or Woman) of God,

In every generation, ministers face distractions that threaten to displace what is most essential. Administrative pressures, congregational expectations, and personal burdens often crowd the schedule until the urgent overshadows the eternal. Yet none of these responsibilities, however legitimate, can replace the foundational discipline of prayer. Prayer is not devotional sentiment reserved for quiet moments; it is the ordained means of communion between God and His servants. A ministry untethered from prayer will inevitably drift from doctrinal fidelity and spiritual vitality. Preaching may continue outwardly, outlines may remain organized, and schedules may stay full, but authority diminishes when communion weakens.

Scripture reveals that prayer is precious before God. It is not discarded once spoken but preserved in His presence, as Revelation 5:8 declares. The minister must therefore learn to pause the demands of life and deliberately enter the presence of the Lord. Before one speaks publicly for God, one must first speak privately with Him. The incense must rise before the sermon does.

With Love From Above,

A Failure to Communicate

There have been seasons in my own ministry when prayer was neglected under the pressure of responsibility. During those periods, I attempted to sustain spiritual work with diminished spiritual strength. What felt like exhaustion was often the consequence of insufficient communion. The sermons were structured, the outlines complete, and the illustrations prepared, yet something essential was absent. Prayerlessness does not always produce immediate collapse; more often it produces gradual erosion. Authority thins, compassion fades, boldness weakens, study becomes mechanical, and what is sacred quietly becomes routine.

Prayer is not episodic, nor is it reserved for crisis or ceremony. It is daily dependence. To grasp its gravity, we look to the Old Testament altar of incense, where the Lord established a pattern that still instructs the preacher today.

The Altar of Prayer

"And Aaron shall burn thereon sweet incense every morning... a perpetual incense before the LORD throughout your generations" (Exodus 30:7–8). The altar of incense provides a theological framework for understanding prayer in ministry.

First, it was perpetual. The incense ascended continually, morning and evening, before the Lord. Prayer is not an accessory to ministry; it is its atmosphere. The New Testament echoes this rhythm when believers are commanded to "pray without ceasing." The preacher who waits until Saturday evening to pray over Sunday's message has misunderstood communion's cadence. Prayer must precede preparation, accompany preparation, and follow proclamation. Preaching not sustained by prayer may inform the mind, but it rarely pierces the heart. A sermon born in study alone may instruct, yet a sermon born in study and prayer carries transforming weight.

Second, it was pure. The Lord warned, "Ye shall offer no strange incense thereon" (Exodus 30:9). The composition of the incense was specified and set apart for holy use. It was not to be altered or imitated for common purposes. Prayer must likewise remain undiluted by self-interest, pride, or performance. The minister who prays merely to develop content rather than to seek God Himself risks offering strange incense. Public eloquence without private communion shifts from worship to display. Therefore, we must ask whether we are praying for power or for prominence, for God's glory or for personal success. Both prayers are heard, but only one rises as sweet incense.

Third, it was purposeful. The altar of incense was distinct from other sacrifices, with defined boundaries and a defined function. Positioned before the veil near the Most Holy Place, it symbolized proximity without presumption. Prayer is not a substitute for study, nor is study a substitute for prayer. Study fills the mind while prayer softens the heart. Study without prayer produces cold orthodoxy, and prayer without study produces unstable zeal. When both unite, conviction and clarity meet in holy balance.

Fourth, it was grounded in atonement. Once a year, blood was applied to the horns of the altar (Exodus 30:10), reminding Israel that access to God was covenantal, not casual. Today, Christ Himself is our propitiation. We approach not on the merit of office but on the merit of the Cross. We do not pray because we are pastors; we pray because we are redeemed. Every petition ascends through blood-bought access, and every sermon delivered must remember the price that secured that privilege.

The Odours of the Elders

Revelation 5:8 depicts golden vials full of odours, identified as the prayers of the saints. Prayer is not wasted; it is stored. Heaven does not discard what earth forgets. If our prayers are preserved before the throne, negligence in prayer is not a minor oversight but a forfeited privilege. The pulpit is not common ground; it is sacred space. To ascend it without prayerful preparation risks speaking from flesh rather than from communion.

The Order of Acts 6

Acts 6:4 records the apostles declaring, "We will give ourselves continually to prayer, and to the ministry of the word." The order is deliberate. Prayer preceded Word ministry. The early church understood that proclamation without communion was incomplete. Word ministry fueled by prayer produces courage, clarity, and conviction. The preacher who prays first inevitably preaches differently, for his message has been shaped in the presence of God before it is spoken before men.

Practical Counsel for the Minister

If prayer has thinned in your life, do not wait for crisis to restore it. Begin deliberately and without spectacle. Guard a daily hour, however modest, and treat it as immovable. Pray over the text before outlining it, asking not merely for insight but for illumination. Pray for specific members of your congregation by name, carrying their burdens before the Lord. Pray after preaching, entrusting visible and invisible results to God. Above all, pray when no one sees. Measure prayer not by emotional intensity but by faithful consistency, for consistency outweighs spectacle and sustains longevity.

Final Encouragement

Even where correction is needed, discouragement is unwarranted. The adversary delights in magnifying minor failures into paralyzing guilt. Instead of retreating in shame, return to the altar. The incense can rise again, communion can be restored, authority can be renewed, and joy can be recovered. Preaching rooted in prayer will endure beyond personality and outlast circumstance. When the incense ascends before the throne, the Word that follows will not return void. Return to the altar and let the incense rise.

Pastoral Charge

Guard your prayer life as fiercely as you guard your doctrine. Your congregation hears your sermons, but God hears your prayers. One reveals your theology; the other reveals your dependence. Do not reverse the order established in Acts 6. Give yourself first to prayer and then to the ministry of the Word. A praying preacher is a powerful preacher, not because of volume or personality, but because of communion.

Study & Reflection

Examine whether your prayer life has become reactive rather than consistent. Consider whether you pray before studying or only after finishing your outline. Reflect on whether you have mistaken preparation for communion and whether mixed motives have crept into your petitions. Ask yourself if you regularly pray for your congregation by name and whether your preaching would change if your prayer life deepened. Write a paragraph identifying one specific adjustment you must make in your prayer discipline this month and outline how you will implement it.

For group discussion, consider why Acts 6 places prayer before Word ministry and how prayer guards against pride in preaching. Discuss common modern distractions that erode prayer and explore how accountability can strengthen a minister's devotional life. Reflect on the danger of professionalized preaching and how the imagery of incense deepens our understanding of prayer's holiness and privilege.

Ministry Workshop

For your next sermon, practice prayer-first preparation by spending dedicated time praying through the passage before outlining it. Record insights that surface during communion and then begin structured study, noting any difference in tone or emphasis. Over the course of seven days, track time spent in prayer, the focus of those prayers, and distractions encountered, then evaluate patterns honestly. Additionally, select ten members of your congregation and intercede specifically for their growth, trials, and families, observing how deliberate intercession reshapes your preaching posture toward them.

Prayer Focus

Father, keep me near the altar. Lord Jesus, remind me that access is blood-bought. Holy Spirit, teach me to commune before I communicate. Let my sermons rise from incense. Amen.

CHAPTER 6: Are You Ready to Have a Baby? (The Organic Nature of Preaching)

Dear Man (or Woman) of God,

Preaching is often reduced to mechanical assembly—introduction, outline, conclusion. Structure has value, but Scripture presents the movement of the Word in far more organic terms. Paul described himself as "travailing in birth" for those under his spiritual care (Galatians 4:19). The imagery is not that of construction but of conception, gestation, and delivery. A message must be carried before it can be delivered. We are not manufacturers of sermons; we are stewards of living truth. Do not rush to the pulpit before the Word has taken root in your own soul.

With Love From Above,
The Penman Preacher

The Miracle of Spiritual Reproduction

The incarnation of Christ provides a theological pattern for understanding preaching. The Word entered the world not through human engineering but through divine initiative, for "the Word was made flesh" (John 1:14). Authentic preaching likewise originates with God. We do not invent truth; we receive it, believe it, carry it, and ultimately deliver it. When preaching becomes mechanical, it loses vitality. When it remains organic—born of revelation, faith, grace, and Christ-centered formation—it carries life. This process can be understood in seven stages of spiritual development that mirror the imagery of birth.

Reception — Hearing the Word

Mary first received the message before she carried the child (Luke 1:26–38). The process began with revelation. Preaching must begin with Scripture. Authority does not originate in personality, innovation, emotional intensity, or cultural relevance. It originates in the written Word of God. Without a clear "Thus saith the Lord," there is no legitimate conception. If the text has not spoken, the preacher has no authority to speak. Reception requires humility. Before we stand over the Word to proclaim it, we must sit under it to receive it.

Conception — Believing the Word

When Mary responded, "Be it unto me according to thy word," the message moved from hearing to believing. Information became conviction. The preacher must believe the message personally before proclaiming it publicly. It is possible to exegete a passage without embracing it and to outline truth without submitting to it. Yet preaching without personal conviction produces sterile proclamation. Conception occurs when the preacher says, "Lord, let this Word live in me first." Only then does the message move from the page into the heart.

Gestation — Hidden Formation

Growth within the womb was not engineered by Mary's effort; it unfolded quietly and steadily over time. Likewise, the development of a sermon involves hidden seasons of study, meditation, correction, and prayer. Much of what God performs in a minister is unseen by others. Gestation requires patience. The temptation is to rush; the discipline is to wait. Some messages form quickly, while others require extended meditation. Do not despise the hidden months, for what is unseen often determines what will later be powerful. Depth is rarely formed in haste.

Quickening — Life Becomes Evident

When Mary encountered Elisabeth, the child leaped in her womb (Luke 1:41). Life became evident. In sermon preparation, there is often a moment when the message ceases to be abstract and becomes alive. Clarity sharpens, the burden deepens, and the focus centers unmistakably upon Christ. Every sermon must ultimately converge upon Him. If Christ is absent, the message may be moral, practical, or motivational, but it is not fully Christian preaching. Christ is not an accessory added at the conclusion; He is the heartbeat from which the message draws life. When the sermon quickens around Him, you will sense it.

Expectation — Waiting on Timing

The months preceding birth required endurance and quiet trust. Growth was gradual and largely invisible. The minister likewise learns to wait upon God's timing. Not every message is delivered immediately. Some burdens are carried for weeks. Some themes return repeatedly, and some texts deepen over years. Expectation cultivates patience and guards against impatience disguised as zeal. Trust the timing of God. He knows when the message is ready to be revealed.

Delivery — Public Proclamation

What was formed in secret is unveiled publicly. Delivery is not performance; it is revelation. The preacher does not create life in the moment of proclamation; he reveals what God has already formed within him. If gestation has been shallow, delivery will be strained. If formation has been thorough, proclamation will carry weight. Volume must never be confused with vitality. The strength of delivery depends upon the depth of prior formation. What is born in prayer will speak with authority in the pulpit.

Presentation — Glory Directed Upward

When Christ was born, the angels directed glory heavenward (Luke 2:14). Likewise, preaching must culminate not in admiration for the messenger but in worship of God. If a congregation leaves impressed with the preacher yet unchanged by the message, something essential has been misplaced. Healthy spiritual birth results in glory directed upward. The aim of preaching is not applause but adoration.

The Danger of Premature Delivery

There is such a thing as spiritual prematurity. When eagerness to speak outpaces spiritual preparation, strain inevitably follows. A sermon may be technically sound yet spiritually thin. Premature delivery often reveals insufficient prayer, shallow meditation, borrowed conviction, or imitated tone. Spiritual life cannot be rushed into maturity. Let the Word mature within you before attempting to mature others. Time invested in formation safeguards the fruit of proclamation.

A Personal Reflection

There was a season in my ministry when eagerness to speak exceeded spiritual preparation. The result was difficulty that exposed deficiencies in prayer and patience. I mistook movement for maturity and preparation for formation. What felt like defeat became instruction. God often allows humbling seasons to remind His servants that spiritual birth cannot be rushed. The Word must be carried before it is delivered, and humility is often learned in the waiting.

Marks of a Mature Message

A sermon has matured when it has corrected you before you attempt to correct others, comforted you before you comfort others, and convicted you before you confront others. It consistently points to Christ and produces humility rather than pride. When the message has done its work in you, it is ready to do its work through you. Formation precedes fruitful proclamation.

Final Encouragement

Do not measure fruit too quickly. A mother does not question the value of gestation simply because birth is not immediate. Growth is occurring even when unseen. Carry the Word carefully, nurture it prayerfully, deliver it faithfully, and give God the glory for the life it brings. What is formed in patience often bears fruit in power.

Pastoral Charge

Do not rush what God is forming. Guard your study, guard your prayer, and guard your patience. The pulpit is not a factory floor; it is a delivery room. Let every sermon be born of Scripture, formed in prayer, centered on Christ, and offered for God's glory. When preaching remains organic, it remains alive.

Study & Reflection

Examine whether you treat sermon preparation as mechanical assembly or spiritual formation. Consider whether the Word has corrected you before you attempt to correct others and whether schedule pressure tempts you toward premature delivery. Reflect on whether Christ is clearly central in your messages and where you may have experienced premature delivery in ministry. Identify the message God is currently forming within you and write a paragraph describing what stage of development you are presently in with your next sermon.

For group discussion, explore why Paul employed birth imagery for spiritual ministry and what dangers arise when preaching becomes mechanical. Consider practical ways to allow proper gestation and how pride may tempt a preacher toward premature delivery. Discuss what distinguishes performance from proclamation and how directing glory to God guards the preacher's heart.

Ministry Workshop

Select a recent sermon and trace its development from initial burden to final delivery. Identify when conviction deepened, when clarity arrived, and how Christ became central. Evaluate whether proper gestation occurred. Next, review your most recent outline and underline every explicit or implicit reference to Christ. If He were removed, would the sermon collapse? If not, refine accordingly. Finally, journal the organic development of your next message, noting how the text corrects you personally, when moments of conviction arise, and when the sense of quickening becomes evident. Track the process intentionally and prayerfully.

Prayer Focus

Father, form the Word in me before You form it through me. Lord Jesus, be the center of every message. Holy Spirit, grant patience in preparation and humility in delivery. Let every sermon bring glory to God. Amen.

CHAPTER 7: THE FIVE SOLAS

The Foundation Beneath the Fire

Primary Text

Colossians 2:6–7 – "Therefore, as you received Christ Jesus the Lord, so walk in Him, rooted and built up in Him, strengthened in the faith as you were taught, and overflowing with thankfulness."

Dear Man (or Woman) of God,

We have traced Christ through Scripture, carried the Word before delivering it, and sought to honor Him in every message. But what sustains the fire in ministry? Foundation. Not personality, preference, or tradition — but truth.

The Five Solas of the Reformation are more than history; they are the theological backbone beneath faithful preaching:

- Sola Scriptura — Scripture Alone: Scripture is our final authority. Preaching is not performance; it is proclamation.
- Sola Fide — Faith Alone: Justification comes through faith, not effort. Preach trust, not admiration.

- Sola Gratia — Grace Alone: Salvation is God's initiative from beginning to end. Proclaim grace, not self-improvement.
- Solus Christus — Christ Alone: Christ is the center and substance of all preaching.
- Soli Deo Gloria — To God Alone Be Glory: Every act of ministry points to God's glory, not applause.

Emotion without doctrine burns out. Doctrine without devotion dries up. But those rooted and built up in Christ are strengthened in the faith and overflow with thankfulness. Stand on Scripture, stand by faith, stand in grace, stand in Christ, and stand for God's glory.

Study & Reflection

Reflect on your ministry foundation. Ask yourself:
- Am I truly rooted and built up in Christ in my study, preaching, and prayer?
- Does Scripture alone guide my preparation and delivery?
- Are faith, grace, and Christ central in every message?
- Does my ministry aim for God's glory above personal recognition?

Write a paragraph describing how your ministry reflects these foundational truths and where your "fire" may need refueling in Christ.

Ministry Workshop

Select a recent sermon or teaching series and evaluate it:

- Where was Scripture supreme in shaping your message?
- Was faith and grace clearly communicated as God's work, not your effort?
- Was Christ unmistakably central, and did the sermon point to God's glory?

Next, journal your next message with intentional attention to being rooted and built up in Christ: track Scripture's shaping of your preparation, faith guiding your delivery, grace informing your tone, Christ remaining central, and God receiving glory.

Prayer Focus

Father, root my ministry in Christ alone. Lord Jesus, strengthen me in faith, and let every message point to Your glory. Holy Spirit, guide my preparation, fuel my passion, and overflow my ministry with thankfulness. Amen.

CHAPTER 8

THE YEAR OF JUBILEE

Resetting What Has Drifted

Primary Text: Leviticus 25

Dear Man (or Woman) of God,

There are dangers in ministry that do not arrive with alarm. They do not announce themselves through scandal or collapse. They move quietly, settling into routine and disguising themselves as stability. The sermons are still prepared. The services are still conducted. The congregation still gathers. Yet beneath the visible structure something has shifted. Zeal has cooled into familiarity. Dependence has thinned into habit. Conviction has softened into efficiency. This is not open rebellion. It is subtle drift.

In Leviticus 25, the Lord established the Year of Jubilee as a covenant safeguard against drift. Every fiftieth year the trumpet would sound, debts would be released, servants would be freed, and inherited land would return to its original family. Jubilee was not emotional revivalism; it was structured restoration. It was a divinely appointed interruption built into the life of the nation to prevent permanent imbalance and quiet accumulation. The Lord declared plainly that the land belonged to Him. Israel were stewards, not ultimate owners. Their possession was real, but it was conditional and accountable.

The theology beneath Jubilee confronts the preacher. Ministry ground does not belong to you. The pulpit is not your inheritance to control. The congregation is not your possession to manage as personal property. The fruit is not your achievement to preserve. When stewardship subtly shifts into ownership, pressure increases, pride grows, and fear of loss begins to govern decisions. Jubilee dismantles that illusion. It forces return. It reminds the steward of the Owner.

Drift in ministry often begins not with false doctrine but with diminished devotion. You prepare sermons without trembling. You preach truths that no longer arrest your own heart. Prayer becomes procedural rather than dependent. Success becomes measurable in attendance rather than obedience. You guard reputation more carefully than holiness. Nothing collapses overnight, but something erodes slowly. Jubilee confronts erosion before collapse becomes necessary.

Reset is not weakness; it is obedience. The Lord built mercy into the rhythm of Israel's life because He knew debt would accumulate and imbalance would grow. Likewise, He knows the preacher's frame. He knows fatigue layers quietly. He knows disappointments linger. He knows how comparison creeps in and how subtle pride hardens the heart. Resetting before Him is humility, not retreat.

Jubilee ultimately points beyond agricultural rhythms. It whispers toward Christ. True liberty does not arrive every fifty years; it arrived at the Cross. The release of debt, the restoration of inheritance, the freedom from bondage—all find their fulfillment in Him. Jubilee was shadow; Christ is substance. When you reset your ministry, you are not returning to nostalgia. You are returning to Christ-centered dependence.

Examine yourself honestly. Has study become mechanical? Has preaching grown predictable? Has tenderness under conviction diminished? Have you begun to protect position more than purity? Drift rarely announces itself to the preacher first, but heaven sees. Let the trumpet sound in your own heart before you presume to sound it publicly. Build rhythms of recalibration. Withdraw when needed. Confess quickly. Invite correction. Remember whose field you stand in. Reset before you drift beyond recognition.

Pastoral Charge

Do not wait for crisis to reset your ministry. Guard your study, guard your prayer, and guard your dependence on God. The pulpit is not a stage for personal pride; it is a stewardship entrusted by the Lord. Let every sermon, every act of leadership, and every moment of ministry be rooted in

Scripture, bathed in prayer, and surrendered to Christ. When ministry is stewarded rightly, it remains alive and fruitful.

Study & Reflection

Examine your own ministry rhythms. Consider whether your devotion has drifted into routine, your prayer into procedure, or your preaching into habit. Ask yourself:

- Has my preparation become mechanical rather than spiritual?
- Do I allow Scripture to correct me before I attempt to correct others?
- Am I guarding against premature delivery of messages or decisions?
- Is Christ truly central in my sermons and leadership, or do I lean on method, reputation, or schedule?

Write a paragraph describing areas where you sense subtle drift in your heart, sermons, or leadership, and note where the Lord may be calling you to reset.

Ministry Workshop

Select a recent sermon or teaching series and trace its development from initial burden to final delivery. Identify:

- When conviction first deepened in your heart.
- When clarity emerged through study or prayer.
- How Christ became central in the message.

- Whether any part of your preparation or delivery was rushed or mechanical.

Next, journal your next message, tracking how the Scripture corrects you personally, when moments of conviction arise, and how the sense of spiritual "reset" becomes evident. Evaluate whether each step reflects dependence on God rather than mere habit or efficiency.

Prayer Focus

Father, restore what has drifted and reset my heart to You. Lord Jesus, center every message and every act of ministry on Yourself. Holy Spirit, cultivate humility, patience, and dependence in me. Let every sermon, every service, and

CHAPTER 9

THE SOUND OF THE TRUMPET

Announcing Liberty Clearly

Primary Text: Leviticus 25:9–10

Dear Man (or Woman) of God,

Liberty in Israel was never assumed; it was proclaimed. The trumpet of Jubilee did not whisper across the land. It sounded clearly, cutting through routine and interrupting normalcy. The command was direct: "Thou shalt cause the trumpet of the jubile to sound." The clarity was not optional. Preacher, ambiguity has never set captives free.

The trumpet was blown on the Day of Atonement. That detail anchors the proclamation in sacrifice. Liberty flowed from blood. Freedom was not detached optimism; it was covenant mercy rooted in substitution. In the same way, gospel proclamation must remain inseparable from the Cross. If Christ crucified is not central, liberty becomes sentimental language rather than redemptive reality.

Proclaim liberty. Not imply it. Not assume it. Proclaim it. Clarity in preaching is not harshness; it is love. If sin is undefined, repentance is impossible. If judgment is softened, grace is minimized. If the Cross is generalized, faith becomes confused. Your people must understand what they are saved from, who alone saves, why salvation was necessary, and how salvation is received. Vagueness comforts the bound. Clarity confronts the bound.

Scripture warns that if the trumpet gives an uncertain sound, who shall prepare for battle? An uncertain gospel produces uncertain converts. When repentance is rebranded as personal growth, when holiness is treated as optional, when the exclusivity of Christ is softened into suggestion, the trumpet becomes noise. Noise does not awaken the sleeping.

You will feel pressure to soften. The age prefers tone over truth and comfort over conviction. You will be tempted to minimize warnings of judgment and avoid doctrines that unsettle. But unclear warning is not compassion. It is negligence. If a watchman sees danger and whispers, he is not gentle; he is unfaithful.

Clarity does not require cruelty. The trumpet is loud but not malicious. Speak plainly. Define carefully. Proclaim courageously. Let conviction arise from the Word rather than from personality. Review your preaching honestly. Is the gospel unmistakable? Is repentance explained? Is Christ exalted as the only remedy? Could a searching sinner understand how to be reconciled to God? Let your trumpet carry a certain sound rooted firmly in the Cross.

Pastoral Charge

Do not whisper when God calls you to sound the trumpet. Guard clarity, guard fidelity, and guard the centrality of Christ. The pulpit is not a suggestion box; it is a proclamation station. Let every sermon and every act of ministry announce liberty clearly, rooted in the Cross, and unambiguous in its message. When preaching is faithful, it awakens the bound and guides the lost.

Study & Reflection

Examine your preaching and teaching for clarity. Consider whether your messages are unmistakably gospel-centered or softened for comfort. Ask yourself:

- Do I proclaim liberty, or merely imply it?
- Is repentance clearly defined, and Christ exalted as the only remedy?
- Do I avoid necessary warnings to protect favor, or do I speak truth in love?
- Would a searching sinner understand how to be reconciled to God from my sermons alone?

Write a paragraph reflecting on areas where your proclamation may have become uncertain or ambiguous, and where God is calling you to sharpen your trumpet.

Ministry Workshop

Select a recent sermon or teaching series and trace how clearly the gospel was communicated. Identify:

- Where liberty was proclaimed with clarity.
- Where ambiguity or vagueness might have crept in.
- How Christ was presented as the central remedy.
- Any moments where conviction arose directly from Scripture rather than from style or personality.

Next, journal your next message, intentionally tracking how each point of the gospel is communicated clearly. Note when the Word convicts hearts, when the message resists dilution, and how faithful proclamation brings clarity to the listeners.

Prayer Focus

Father, let my trumpet sound with clarity. Lord Jesus, make Christ unmistakable in every message. Holy Spirit, sharpen my words, protect fidelity, and grant courage to proclaim liberty boldly. Let every sermon awaken the bound and glorify Your Name. Amen.

CHAPTER 10

RETURNING TO YOUR POSSESSION

Recovering What Was Lost

Primary Text: Leviticus 25:13

Dear Man (or Woman) of God,

"In the year of this jubile ye shall return every man unto his possession." Jubilee was not merely release; it was restoration. What had been temporarily transferred was returned. What had been diminished was recovered. Some ministers do not need a new calling; they need a return.

Over time familiarity dulls wonder. You still affirm the gospel, but you no longer marvel at it. You still prepare sermons, but you no longer linger in worship. Complexity increases while simplicity fades. Programs expand while prayer shortens. Activity multiplies while intimacy thins. You have not abandoned truth; you have drifted from possession.

Return to private worship. Return to slow meditation. Return to unhurried prayer. Return to joyful study. Complication often masquerades as maturity, yet the power has always been in the Word, the Cross, the Spirit, and the gospel itself. You cannot lead others back to wonder if you have not returned yourself.

Returning requires humility. It requires admitting that something precious has grown distant. It may require repentance from subtle pride, from overconfidence, from self-reliance disguised as competence. Jubilee teaches that restoration is not shameful; it is covenant mercy.

Ask yourself when you felt most alive in ministry. What marked that season? Dependence? Simplicity? Awe? Those elements were not immature; they were foundational. Returning is not regression. It is realignment. Recover what was lost before it becomes memory rather than possession.

CHAPTER 11

SERVANTS SET FREE

Grace That Restores, Not Exploits

Primary Text: Leviticus 25:39–41

Dear Man (or Woman) of God,

In Jubilee, servants were released. No Israelite was to be permanently enslaved. The covenant refused to sanctify lifelong bondage among brothers. This principle speaks directly to pastoral authority. The shepherd must never become a master.

You carry authority, but it is delegated. The people entrusted to your care belong to Christ. When leadership subtly shifts from stewardship to control, grace is compromised. It is possible to preach freedom while cultivating dependency. It is possible to proclaim Christ's lordship while quietly building personal loyalty.

Watch for manipulative language. Watch for fear-based motivation. Watch for environments where questioning is discouraged and personality replaces Scripture as the central reference point. Grace restores; it does not dominate. True shepherding feeds, protects, and guides without possessing.

Authority exercised with humility reflects the Chief Shepherd. Authority exercised for ego distorts Him. If your people grow in dependence upon Christ rather than dependence upon you, you are succeeding. If they mature beyond your direct influence while remaining faithful to the Word, you have shepherded well.

Jubilee reminds the preacher that no servant of God should be trapped under spiritual exploitation. Lead firmly when Scripture demands it, but always with the awareness that you too are a servant under authority. Shepherd, do not own.

Pastoral Charge

Do not mistake drift for progress. Guard your wonder, guard your dependence, and guard your intimacy with God. The pulpit is not merely a platform for activity; it is a place of restoration. Let every sermon, every act of ministry, and every moment of preparation reflect a return to your possession in Christ. When ministry is restored, it carries life and power.

Study & Reflection

Examine your ministry life for what may have been lost to familiarity or routine. Ask yourself:
- Have I drifted from private worship, meditation, or unhurried prayer?

- Do I still marvel at the gospel, or has routine dulled awe?
- Are my sermons prepared out of devotion or mere duty?
- Where has complexity replaced simplicity, and activity replaced intimacy with God?

Write a paragraph describing the areas in your life and ministry that need restoration. Reflect on what "returning" would look like for you personally.

Ministry Workshop

Select a recent ministry activity, sermon, or devotional time and trace whether it reflected restoration or routine. Identify:

- When dependence on God was evident.
- When simplicity and awe were present.
- When ministry felt vibrant versus mechanical.
- Where restoration or realignment is needed before moving forward.

Next, journal your next message or devotional time, intentionally returning to the practices and attitudes that restore wonder, dependence, and intimacy. Track your engagement with the Word, prayer, and Christ-centered preparation, noting where restoration has taken root.

Prayer Focus

Father, restore what has been lost in me. Lord Jesus Father, restore what has been lost in me. Lord Jesus, renew my awe for Your gospel. Holy Spirit, revive my dependence, simplicity, and intimacy with You. Let my ministry reflect restoration, and let every word and act bring glory to Your Name. Amen.

CHAPTER 12

THE WATCHMAN'S WARNING

If Thou Dost Not Speak

Primary Text: Ezekiel 33:6–9

Dear Man (or Woman) of God,

The watchman stood on the wall not to create danger but to observe it. If he saw the sword coming and did not blow the trumpet, the blood of the people was required at his hand. The responsibility was clear. He was not accountable for the enemy's existence. He was accountable for sounding the warning.

This is a sobering parallel for the preacher. You are not responsible for the hardness of hearts. You are not responsible for outcomes. But you are responsible to speak what you see in the Word. Silence in the presence of clear truth is not neutrality; it is participation in loss.

The temptation to remain silent is real. You will face resistance. You will encounter misunderstanding. You may experience rejection. Yet faithfulness is not measured by applause but by obedience. The watchman who warns and is ignored is still faithful. The watchman who remains silent to preserve comfort is not.

Preach sin plainly. Preach judgment honestly. Preach Christ boldly. Preach grace freely. Do not weaponize truth, but do not withhold it. Speak with tears if necessary, but speak. One day you will stand before the Chief Shepherd, not to answer for popularity or influence, but for faithfulness. The question will not be how large your ministry became, but whether you warned clearly and proclaimed truthfully.

See clearly. Speak faithfully. Stand humbly. Blow the trumpet. Leave the results with God.

Pastoral Charge

Do not remain silent when God calls you to speak. Guard your courage, guard your fidelity, and guard the clarity of the Word. The pulpit is not a stage for comfort; it is a watchtower for warning. Let every sermon, every exhortation, and every act of ministry reflect faithful proclamation. When ministry is faithful, lives are warned, and truth is honored.

Study & Reflection

Examine your preaching and teaching for faithfulness. Ask yourself:

- Have I avoided difficult truths to preserve comfort or favor?

- Do I speak sin plainly, judgment honestly, and Christ boldly?
- Am I accountable to God for clarity, regardless of response or outcome?
- Where has fear or approval-seeking silenced necessary warnings?

Write a paragraph reflecting on areas where you may have remained silent or softened truth. Consider how God is calling you to faithful proclamation.

Ministry Workshop

Select a recent sermon or teaching moment and trace whether you spoke faithfully. Identify:
- Moments when truth was clearly proclaimed.
- Points where you may have withheld warning or correction.
- How Christ-centered grace accompanied the message.
Where courage or clarity could be strengthened in future messages.

Next, journal your next sermon or teaching series, intentionally tracking where God calls you to warn clearly and speak truthfully. Note when conviction arises in you and when your responsibility as watchman is faithfully exercised.

Prayer Focus

Father, grant me courage to speak when it is difficult. Lord Jesus, center every warning in Your truth and grace. Holy Spirit, sharpen my clarity, strengthen my obedience, and guide my proclamation. Let every message honor You and warn faithfully, leaving outcomes in Your hands. Amen.

CONCLUSION:

Put Down the Pen

Throughout this book, we have examined preaching through many lenses—gold mining, crosshairs, incense, birth, foundation. Each metaphor has illuminated the sacred calling to handle the Word of God rightly, studying to show ourselves approved (2 Timothy 2:15). Yet there comes a moment when every metaphor must give way to surrender.

The temptation for the preacher—especially one who loves structure and language—is to believe that the power lies in the pen. But if Scripture alone is our authority, then we are stewards, not authors. If faith alone justifies (Romans 5:1), our persuasion does not convert. If grace alone saves (Ephesians 2:8 9), our effort does not regenerate. If Christ alone mediates (1 Timothy 2:5), we are not the bridge between God and man. And if all things are of Him and to Him (Romans 11:36), the glory was never ours to claim.

The pen is a tool. It is not the source.

There is a holy tension in ministry. We are commanded to preach the Word (2 Timothy 4:2). We are called to abide in Christ, for without Him we can do nothing (John 15:5). But never are we told to manufacture power. At some point, every faithful preacher must lay the manuscript down and pray, "Lord, unless Thou speakest, nothing eternal will happen."

This is not a call to laziness; it is a call to dependence.

But dependence does not mean delay. Exhort one another daily, while it is called Today (Hebrews 3:13). There are seasons when truth is softened and conviction exchanged for approval. This must not be one of them. The cross is still the power of God (1 Corinthians 1:18). Christ is risen indeed — the firstfruits of them that slept (1 Corinthians 15:20). His grace is sufficient (2 Corinthians 12:9).

Preach now. Pray now. Stand now.

If Christ is risen, He must be exalted. If grace is sufficient, it must be declared. If faith saves, it must be called for. If the glory belongs to God, we must not compete for it.

You may never preach beyond your county line. Yet if you faithfully handle the Word where you are, eternity will not overlook it. The assistant pastor, the teacher, the evangelist, the shepherd — all stand beneath the same authority and under the same grace.

And when the sermon is finished, when the outline is complete, when the final word is written, there is only one faithful posture left:

Put down the pen. Bow your head. Ask for fire.

Then rise — and preach while it is called today.

Let the Word stand. Let Christ be seen. Let God receive the glory. And let the pulpit burn — not with personality, but with truth.

SCRIPTURE INDEX

(Text – Theme)

OLD TESTAMENT

Genesis
1:1 — Creation; The Beginning
1:26 — Image of God
2:7 — Breath of Life
6:5 — Sinfulness of Man
50:20 — Providence; Sovereignty

Exodus
4:12 — Divine Enablement

Deuteronomy
6:4 — The Oneness of God

Joshua
1:8 — Meditation; Obedience; Prosperity

1 Samuel
16:7 — The Heart; Divine Perspective

2 Chronicles
7:14 — Repentance; National Healing

Job
14:14 — Resurrection Hope
19:25 — Redeemer; Assurance

Psalm
8:4 — The Value of Man
23:1 — The Lord Our Shepherd
23:4 — Comfort in the Valley
27:1 — Light and Salvation
46:1 — Refuge and Strength
51:10 — Renewal; Clean Heart
100:5 — Goodness of God
119:105 — The Word as Light

Proverbs
3:5–6 — Trust; Divine Direction
18:21 — Power of the Tongue

Ecclesiastes
3:1 — Seasons of Life

Isaiah
9:6 — The Promised Messiah
26:3 — Perfect Peace
40:31 — Renewed Strength
53:5 — Atonement; Suffering Servant

Jeremiah
1:5 — Divine Calling
29:11 — Hope and Future
33:3 — Prayer; Revelation

Lamentations
3:22–23 — Mercy; Faithfulness

Ezekiel
37:5 — Spiritual Revival

Daniel
12:3 — Eternal Reward

Micah
6:8 — Justice; Mercy; Humility

Habakkuk
2:2 — Vision; Clarity

Zechariah
4:6 — Power of the Spirit

Malachi
3:6 — Immutability of God

NEW TESTAMENT

Matthew
5:16 — Witness; Good Works
6:33 — Kingdom Priority
11:28 — Rest in Christ
22:37 — Greatest Commandment

Mark
9:23 — Faith

Luke
1:37 — Nothing Impossible with God

10:27 — Love God; Love Neighbor

John
1:1 — Deity of Christ
1:14 — Incarnation
3:16 — Salvation; Love of God
8:12 — Light of the World
10:10 — Abundant Life
14:6 — The Only Way
15:5 — Abiding in Christ

Acts
1:8 — Power to Witness
4:12 — Exclusivity of Salvation

Romans
3:23 — Universal Sin
5:8 — Demonstrated Love
8:28 — Divine Purpose
8:38–39 — Security in Christ
12:2 — Transformation

1 Corinthians
10:13 — Temptation; Deliverance
13:4–7 — Charity; Love Defined
15:57 — Victory Through Christ

2 Corinthians
5:7 — Walk by Faith
5:17 — New Creation
12:9 — Sufficient Grace

Galatians
2:20 — Crucified with Christ
5:22–23 — Fruit of the Spirit

Ephesians
2:8–9 — Salvation by Grace
3:20 — Exceeding Abundance
6:10–11 — Spiritual Armor

Philippians
1:6 — Confidence in Completion
4:6–7 — Peace of God
4:13 — Strength Through Christ

Colossians
3:23 — Work as unto the Lord

1 Thessalonians
5:16–18 — Rejoice; Pray; Give Thanks

2 Timothy
1:7 — Spirit of Power
3:16 — Inspiration of Scripture

Hebrews
4:12 — Power of the Word
11:1 — Definition of Faith

James
1:5 — Wisdom from God
2:17 — Faith and Works

1 Peter
5:7 — Casting Cares

1 John
1:9 — Confession; Forgiveness
4:4 — Victory Over the World
4:19 — Love Originates in God

Revelation
3:20 — Invitation of Christ
21:4 — Eternal Comfort

www.ingramcontent.com/pod-product-compliance
Lightning Source LLC
LaVergne TN
LVHW090534110826
845146LV00003B/1097

* 9 7 9 8 2 1 8 9 3 7 6 2 1 *